Liquids

Charlotte Deschermeier

PowerKiDS press.

New York

Published in 2014 by The Rosen Publishing Group, Inc.
29 East 21st Street, New York, NY 1001 0

Photo Credits: © 2003-2013 Shutterstock, Inc.

Library of Congress Cataloging-in-Publication Data

Deschermeier, Charlotte, author.
 Liquids / by Charlotte Deschermeier.
    pages cm. – (Ultimate science. Physical science)
 Includes index.
 ISBN 978-1-4777-6077-2 (library) – ISBN 978-1-4777-6078-9 (pbk.) –
 ISBN 978-1-4777-6080-2 (6-pack)
 1. Liquids–Juvenile literature. 2. Matter–Properties–Juvenile literature. I. Title.
 QC145.24.D47 2014
 530.4'2–dc23
                                        2013023582

Manufactured in the United States of America

CPSIA Compliance Information: Batch #W14PK4: For Further Information contact Rosen Publishing, New York, New York at 1-800-237-9932

Contents

Liquid is One State of Matter

All that we see around us is made up of matter. Your house, the food you eat, and even your dog are matter. Matter is usually found in three forms, or states. The three most common states of matter on Earth are gas, liquid, and solid.

All matter is made of tiny parts called **atoms**. They are so small you cannot see them. Atoms join with other atoms to form larger parts called molecules. Millions of molecules connect with each other to form every kind of matter. Solids, liquids, and gases are made up of molecules that are never stationary.

This model of water molecules was made on a computer. It shows how each water molecule includes two hydrogen atoms and one oxygen atom.

These molecules are held together by forces of **attraction**. These forces are called intermolecular forces, or bonds.

The bonds between molecules in a liquid are weaker than those in a solid but stronger than those in gases. Different liquids have certain properties, or characteristics, that allow us to classify them as liquids. Do you know what seawater, soup, and chocolate milk have in common?

One property of water molecules is that they stick together in drops. These drops can join to form puddles or oceans.

Liquids and Volume

There is no fixed shape for a liquid. Instead, it takes the shape of the object holding it. For example, if you poured milk from a tall glass into a short mug, the milk would take on the shape of its new **container**.

The amount of space a liquid fills is called its volume. Although a liquid changes shape to fit its container, its volume remains the same. The volume of milk in the tall glass would be equal to the volume of milk in the mug.

Honey is a thick liquid with strong bonds between its molecules. A liquid's strong intermolecular bonds hold the molecules together and cause its volume to stay the same. The liquid cannot grow larger or become smaller.

It is also possible for liquids to flow. How fast a liquid flows depends on the strength of its intermolecular bonds. For example, honey is a liquid that flows very slowly. It would take a lot longer to fill a cup with honey than it would to fill the same size cup with water. The bonds between the molecules in water are weaker than those in honey.

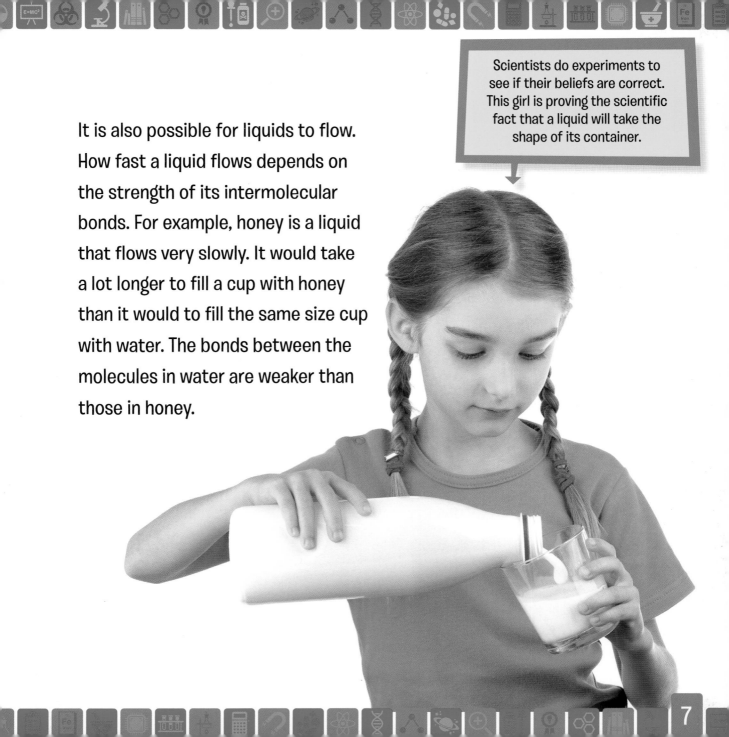

Scientists do experiments to see if their beliefs are correct. This girl is proving the scientific fact that a liquid will take the shape of its container.

Liquids and Cold

There may be puddles of water left on the sidewalk by rain. If the air **temperature** drops, the water may turn to ice. Lowering the temperature of a liquid makes the molecules slow down and move closer together. In time the liquid changes into a solid. This is called freezing. The temperature at which a liquid becomes a solid is its freezing point. At this same temperature, a solid also melts and returns to the liquid state. The freezing point and the melting point of a **substance** are the same temperature.

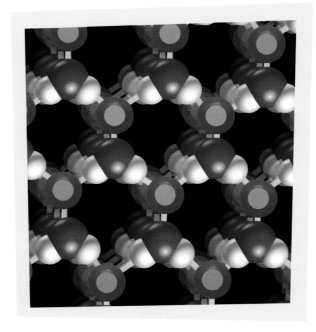

When water molecules freeze, like the ones modeled here, they move closer together.

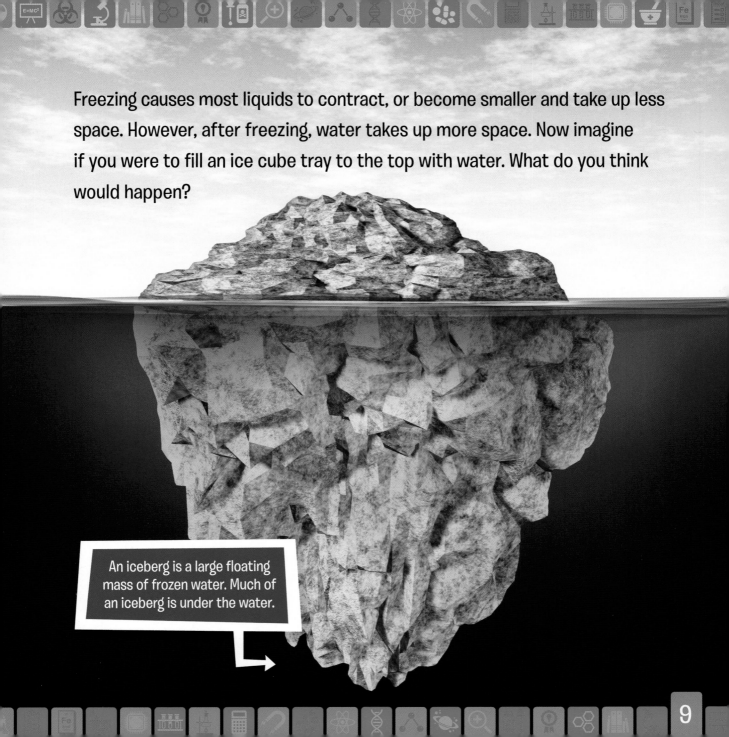

Freezing causes most liquids to contract, or become smaller and take up less space. However, after freezing, water takes up more space. Now imagine if you were to fill an ice cube tray to the top with water. What do you think would happen?

An iceberg is a large floating mass of frozen water. Much of an iceberg is under the water.

Liquids and Heat

A liquid can change into a gas after heating. When a liquid is heated, its molecules take in **energy** from the heat and begin to move faster. The warmer the liquid becomes, the faster the molecules move. As they move around in the liquid, the molecules **collide** with one another. This breaks the intermolecular forces that are holding them together.

The molecules rise from the liquid as bubbles of gas and escape into the air. The liquid molecules are changed into a new state, gas, by the heat.

Once the water molecules break away from one another, they rise from the water's surface as a gas, as shown in this model.

The temperature at which a liquid becomes a gas is different for each liquid. This temperature is called the liquid's boiling point. The boiling point for water is 212°F (100°C). Once a liquid is heated to its boiling point, it cannot get any hotter. If more heat is added to a boiling liquid, this heat changes the liquid into a gas. The liquid does not get any hotter.

The steam that rises from this pot of boiling water is water vapor. Over time all the water in this pot will become vaporized.

Evaporation

Have you ever seen someone boiling a pot of water to make spaghetti? The steam above the pot is water in the form of a gas. When water turns into a gas and enters the air, this is called evaporation. The type of liquid and its temperature determines how quickly a liquid will evaporate.

Hot water evaporates faster than cold water does. For example, a puddle of water on a sidewalk on a hot, sunny day will evaporate much faster than a puddle on a cool, cloudy day.

The molecules in warmer liquids have more energy than cooler liquids. The more energy a molecule has, the faster it moves. When a fast-moving molecule comes near the surface of a liquid, it can break the bonds holding it in the liquid. The molecule then enters the gaseous state.

The amount of a liquid's surface that is **exposed** to the air also has an effect on evaporation. When a liquid can spread out, more molecules in the liquid have a chance to escape and join other molecules in the air. Between water left in a cup and the same amount of water poured out on a cookie sheet, which do you think would evaporate faster?

Wet clothing dries faster on a clothesline than it does if it is left in a pile. More of the clothing's surface is exposed, so the clothing dries faster.

Condensation

Sometimes, the liquid molecules that have changed into gas turn back into liquid. This is called condensation. For example, have you ever noticed that small drops of water form on your window on a cool morning? As air comes in contact with a warmer surface, it can leave tiny drops of water. Liquids that have been mixed together are often separated by scientists using condensation.

The drops of water you find on grass in the morning are called dew. Dew is formed when water molecules that evaporated into the air during a hot summer day cool during the night and condense back into water.

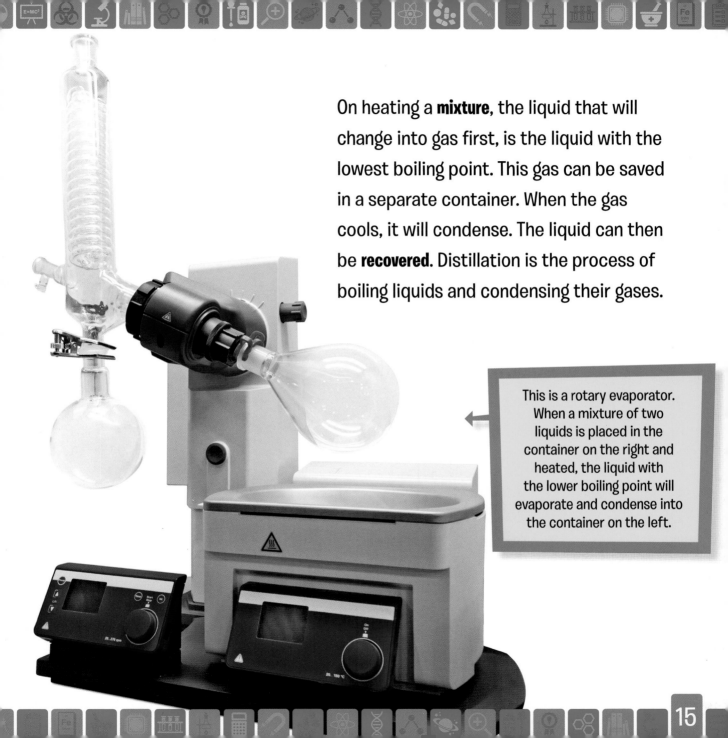

On heating a **mixture**, the liquid that will change into gas first, is the liquid with the lowest boiling point. This gas can be saved in a separate container. When the gas cools, it will condense. The liquid can then be **recovered**. Distillation is the process of boiling liquids and condensing their gases.

This is a rotary evaporator. When a mixture of two liquids is placed in the container on the right and heated, the liquid with the lower boiling point will evaporate and condense into the container on the left.

Liquids in Solutions

When matter is dissolved in a liquid, a solution is created. The liquid is called the solvent. The substance being dissolved is the solute.

Sometimes solutions are made of two liquids mixed together. For example, when you mix chocolate syrup into milk, you have created a solution of chocolate milk. If you are making a solution with two liquids, then the solvent is the liquid you used the most of.

Solute

Solvent

Once the solute is completely full with the solvent, no more solvent can be dissolved. When this occurs the solution is saturated.

The amount of solute that can be dissolved in a solvent depends on the strength of the intermolecular forces of the solute and the solvent. A solute and a solvent that have the same types of intermolecular forces will easily form a solution. Milk and water have intermolecular forces that are alike. They will form a solution easily. Water and oil are not alike. It is not easy for them to form a solution.

Solution

Drop two spoonfuls of ice cream into a glass of milk. Ice cream is the solute, and milk is the solvent.

Special Properties of Liquids

Do you know how bugs can walk across the surface of water? The molecules on the surface of the liquid are attracted to both, the liquid molecules below them and the air molecules above them.

Surface tension keeps this long-legged bug from sinking. This bug is called a water strider. To stride means to take long steps.

Surface tension is caused by the pull of the liquid molecules. This tension tightens up the top of the water and forms a smooth, skin-like covering. Insects use the covering to move across the water.

Strong forces, or bonds, between molecules give liquid molecules the property of cohesion. Cohesion is the ability to stick together. This is why droplets of liquids form round shapes. The drops are round because the liquid molecules clump together.

Mercury is the only metal that is a liquid at room temperature. Mercury, like all liquids, forms round shapes.

Molecules of a liquid are also attracted to the walls of their container. This attraction, known as adhesion, allows a liquid to stick to a solid. Liquids, like water, have the ability to wet paper, wood, and other solids because of adhesion.

Liquids and Density

The amount of matter in a certain volume is called "density" by scientists. Density is how close together the molecules are in a substance. Liquids are usually less dense than solids but more dense than air.

Temperature can change a liquid's density. For example, the molecules in water spread further apart as you increase the temperature.

You need to mix oil and vinegar dressing before sprinkling it on your salad. Over time the oil floats to the top of the bottle because oil is less dense than vinegar is.

Water becomes less dense as the molecules spread further apart. This is why an ice cube floats in a glass of water.

The **physical** property of density helps scientists separate liquids. When two liquids are placed in a container, the denser liquid will fall to the bottom. The less dense liquid will rise to the top. This is why oil floats above vinegar in a bottle of salad dressing before it is shaken. Vinegar is a sour liquid that is used in cooking.

Have you ever seen a lava lamp? As the colored liquid in a lava lamp is heated at the bottom of the lamp, it becomes less dense. The colored liquid then rises to the top and cools, where it becomes slightly more dense. Then it drops to the bottom of the lamp again.

The Most Important Liquid

Most of our planet and our bodies are made up by liquids. Water is Earth's most important liquid. Rivers, lakes, and oceans cover almost three-quarters of Earth's surface.

Our bodies are almost 60 **percent** water by weight. This means that when you step on a scale, water makes up about 60 percent of your weight. Without water, people and other living things cannot live. We now know that most liquids have some physical properties in common. Because water is all around us, we can study its properties to help us understand less familiar liquids. What does water have in common with honey, paint, shampoo, and cooking oil? When you observe liquids and compare their properties, you think like a scientist.

Glossary

atoms (A-temz) The smallest parts of elements that can exist either alone or with other elements.

attraction (uh-TRAK-shun) Pulling something together or toward something else.

collide (kuh-LYD) To crash together.

container (kun-TAY-ner) Something that holds things.

energy (EH-ner-jee) The power to work or to act.

exposed (ik-SPOHZD) Not covered.

mixture (MIKS-cher) A new thing that is made when two or more things are mixed together.

percent (pur-SENT) One part of 100.

physical (FIH-zih-kul) Having to do with natural forces.

recovered (rih-KUH-verd) Got back.

substance (SUB-stans) Any matter that takes up space.

temperature (TEM-pur-cher) How hot or cold something is.

Index

Websites

Due to the changing nature of Internet links, PowerKids Press has developed an online list of websites related to the subject of this book. This site is updated regularly. Please use this link to access the list:

www.powerkidslinks.com/usps/liquid/